This edition published by Barnes & Noble, Inc,
by arrangement with Michelle Lovric
1999 Barnes & Noble Books
ISBN 0-7607-1682-X

LATIN STUFF & NONSENSE
text © 1999 Michelle Lovric & Lea Chambers
concept © 1999 Michelle Lovric, Covent Garden, London
Designed by Michelle Lovric and AB3
Editorial assistants: Kristina Blagojevitch and Nicola Carr
Produced by Imago
Printed and bound in Hong Kong

About the compilers:

Michelle Lovric is the author of *The New York Times* best-seller *Love Letters — AN ANTHOLOGY OF PASSION*. She has previously adapted two 18th-century best-sellers, *The Miseries of Human Life* and *The Scoundrels Dictionary — The Classical Dictionary of the Vulgar Tongue* for Past Times. She worked with Nikiforos Doxiadis Mardas to create a new set of modern translations of Latin and Greek love poetry in her recent title *The Sweetness of Honey and the Sting of Bees, Words of Love from the Ancient Mediterranean* and they also collaborated on *How To Insult, Abuse and Insinuate in Classical Latin*, a witty book of classical invective.

Lea Chambers read Classics at Oxford, and has taught Latin and Ancient Greek for nearly ten years. She is currently Head of Classics at New Hall School. She takes a fresh and innovative approach to teaching the Classics. A talented singer, she often uses musical settings of favorite songs to bring Latin and Ancient Greek to life. For her fortunate pupils, she also translates songs from the pop charts, including the Spice Girls' *Wannabe*. Lea Chambers is married to a Classics teacher and has one child. She lives in Essex.

NG THE PERIOD WHICH THE ACADEMICS STILL PERSIST IN CALLING
HAT RESTRICTED IDIOM WITH ITS LIMITED   MOST
HOUT COLOUR, WITHOUT EVEN LIGHT AND   FLAT
RESQUE EXPRESSIONS OF EARLIER EPOCHS —   ULD,
MMONPLACE   LY RE   Y TH   AND
OLEMNLY T   THE
ALLING PEDA   HAT
RDS TAKING   ER'S HEADS
RS ABOUT BE   GARRULOUS
-THEATRE, M   LL-FITTING,
TES. HE MIGH   NONSENSE
VE PUT UP W   THIS RAG-
HE SHODDY   TERS, WITH
ACCORDING   PEDANTIC
THEIR FORM   NCE TO THE
WAS MECHAN   ESURA AND
SPONDEE. .   AGINATIVE,
TTED WITH   ABLY INTO
PITHET, USED   CATING OR
WITH ITS DUL   NSPEAKABLE
THE ELEPHAN   THE STUPID
OLD CLOWN   HE WAS NO
METAPHORS A   CHICK-PEA;
OTIC PERORA   NGUES, THE
BONED AND R   GNIFICANCE
RMITY OF HIS   THER WITH
UTOLOGY, A   S ESSEINTES.
O HIS TASTE   FOR HE WENT TO   EXTREME,
VITY. HIS UNFORGIVEABLE, UNBELIEVABLE CONSTIPATION. ... HE
R AMONG THOSE WHO FOR SOME REASON ARE THE DELIGHT OF
HAN THE REST. LIVY WHO IS POMPOUS AND SENTIMENTAL, SENECA
ND LYMPHATIC ... JORIS-KARL HUYSMANS, AGAINST NATURE

PATER ROMA REGRESSUS
MIHI HANC PEDICULOSAM
TOGULAM ATTULIT!
*My father went to Rome
and all I got
was this lousy toga!*

LATIN STUFF & NONSENSE

LIMERICKS, PUNS, GRAFFITI, INSULTS, SCHOOLBOY HOWLERS, VERSE AND WORSE

LATIN STUFF & NONSENSE

MICHELLE LOVRIC
& LEA CHAMBERS

BARNES
& NOBLE
BOOKS
NEW YORK

Away with him, away with him!
He speaks Latin.
William Shakespeare, *Henry VI, II*, Act iv, sc. 7

DIES IMPROBI CAPILLI, CARA?
Bad hair day, darling?

Latin is a language
Dead as dead can be;
First it killed the Romans,
Now it's killing me.

All are dead who spoke it,
All are dead who wrote it;
All are dead who learned it —
Lucky dead, they've earned it.
Traditional

Small skill in Latin and still less in Greek
Is more than adequate to all I seek.
William Cowper, English poet, 1731–1800, *Tirocinium*

CONTENTS

Beside 'tis known he could speak Greek,
As naturally as pigs squeak;
That Latin was no more difficile
Than to a blackbird 'tis to whistle.
Samuel Butler, English satirist, 1612–80, *Hudibras*

THE HUMAN BODY

The Sum of its Parts

The human body is a rich source of wit. And Latin
provides a rich sauce for insults, limericks and songs.

VISAS ERAT; HUIC GEMINARUM
DISPAR MODUS AURICULARUM;
MINOR HAEC NIHILI,
PALMA TRIPLICI
IAM FECERAT ALTERA CLARUM.
Translated by P.A. Knox, 1924

There was a young man of Devizes
Whose ears were of different sizes;
The one that was small
Was no use at all,
But the other won several prizes.
Traditional

CORPUS HUMANUM

Body Howlers

The "Schoolboy Howler" — mistranslation or malapropism — is a genre that became popular in the 1920s and 30s, when a whole series of howler books was published. Here are some long-standing favourites, on the subject of the human body. You'll find the correct translations in brackets.

CASUS BELLI	*The lining of the stomach*	*(The fortunes of war)*
DENTE TENACI	*Gnashing his teeth*	*(With a vice-like bite)*
DESERIT COMITEM.	*Its hair fell off.*	*(He abandons his companion.)*
PORTABAT	*He was a gate.*	*(He was carrying)*
GENAE PUELLAE FORMOSAE SUNT.	*Beautiful girls are cheeky.*	*(The girl's cheeks are beautiful.)*
LEGES UTILES HOMINIBUS SUNT.	*Legs are useful to men.*	*(Laws are useful to men.)*
FULMINANTIS MAGNA MANUS IOVIS	*The thundering big hand of Jove*	*(The great hand of Jove the Thunderer)*
ILLI GEMINI ERANT LIBERI QUATTUOR FERE ANNORUM.	*She had twins almost every four years.*	*(Those twins were children almost four years of age.)*
NERVIORUM FINES	*The end of his sinews*	*(The Belgian frontiers)*
DISSENSIT IN TOTO.	*His stomach revolted.*	*(He didn't agree completely.)*

THE BODY

LATA VIDETUR PUGA IN HAC?
Does my bum look big in this?

THAIS HABET NIGROS, NIVEOS LAECANIA DENTES.
QUAE RATIO EST? EMPTOS HAEC HABET, ILLA SUOS.

TOTO VERTICE QUOT GERIT CAPILLOS
ANNOS SI TOT HABET LIGEIA, TRIMA EST.

TOT MEDICAMINIBUS COCTAEQUE SILIGINIS OFFAS
ACCIPIT ET MADIDAE, FACIES DICETUR AN ULCUS?

SCILICET A SPECULI SUMUNTUR IMAGINE FASTUS.

ADIONE PULCHRA EST? IMMO FOEDIUS NIL EST.
QUID ERGO IN ILLA PETITUR ET PLACET? TUSSIT.

CANOVA.

VENUS.

CORPUS

BEAUTIFUL?

Howler:

PRAEDAMQUE IGNARA PUTASSET

*And they in their ignorance took me for a beauty
(And [the tribe] in their ignorance
thought I was booty)*

*Thais has black teeth; Laecania's are white as snow.
The reason? The latter's are shop-bought;
the other's are her own.*
Martial, *Epigrams*, V.43

*The number of hairs on Ligeia's whole head
is a clue to her age.
She's three.*
Martial, *Epigrams*, XII.7

*She plasters on so many curative concoctions —
not least a damp bread face-pack — that you'd be
at a loss to say what she's got underneath, a face
or a festering sore.*
Juvenal, *Satires*, VI

*There's no doubt about it: her ego feasts on
her face in the mirror.*
Ovid, *Amores*, II.17

*Is she really such a beauty? Actually nothing
could be more putrid.
So why is she so sought-after and what does
he see in her?
She has a terminal cough.*
Martial, *Epigrams*, I.10

PULCHRUM ?

CANOVA

DANCING GIRL REPOSING

TAKING A SICK DAY

This original one-act play, set in a doctor's office in Ancient Rome, is
intended to help patients develop a healthy relationship with their G.Ps. It is
written in "pig" Latin, which is best administered orally (i.e. read aloud).

Dramatis Personae: A doctor (Medicus) and a patient (Patientus)

P: est-ne doctor in casa?
M: nonne Popus Catholicus?
P: quaeso pardonem?
M: salve, o patiente.
P: a ... salve, o doctor!
M: nunc ... quid videtur problemus?
P: o doctor. venio directus ad pointum: difficile est mihi in morningibus exsurgere...
M: vis-ne Viagra?
P: exactum.
M: ut, sine dubio, avare es, popularis est — sed non cheapus. non est availibilis in
   Nationali Valetudine.
P: eheu. me miserum. est-ne valde sumptuosus?
M: nonne ursi faciunt caca in silvis?
P: possum hintum capere.
M: erit-ne aliquid elsi?
P: non ... immo ita vero, nunc venis id mentionare.
M: vis-ne certificatum?
P: exactum.
M: accuratius te explorabo. [tollit stethoscopum.] profunde respira! apere os tuum!
   [inspectat tonsillas cum lumine.] scilicet fumas excessivos faggos ... Bensoni
   Saepesque, Silca Scissa et cetera ... moriturus es.
P: nos omnes morituri aliquando ... et nunc venio id cogitare, sum moriens ad faggum...
M: [continuat examinationem] pulsum arteriarum quaeso porrige! nunc tuam
   temperaturam metior.
P: age, o doctor. da mihi directum. noli pulsare circum fruticem!
M: ne minimae quidem notae mali valetudinis. homo validus et robustus es...
P: est impossibile! tu es quaccus. reporto te ad Generalem Medicorum Concilium.
M: ...detecto tamen levem casum doloris "hypochondriacis scivissimi".
P: di immortales! est-ne contagius? est-ne curabilis cum prescriptione? erit-ne possibile
   mihi sportibus ludere?
M: sportibus ludis?
P: ita vero. golfus, actualiter.
M: cur non ita dicis? certificatum per unum vel duos dies?
P: duos. multas gratias.
M: et Viagra ... nugus, nugus, vincus, vincus ... noli amplius dicere. vale.
P: vale, o doctor.

REQUIRO CERTIFICATUM

A Seventeenth-Century "Crepitus" Song

LASCIVE MANUS DABANT ANCILLA ET HEROINA
ET FLATU VENTRIS DECERTABANT QUAE PALMAE SIT REGINA.
JONE LYCHNES TRES ACCENDIT, ET ERECTOS COLLOCABAT,
ET UNO NISU TRES EXSTINXIT, ET ALIO REVOCABAT.
SUA TOTA CUM VIRILI MATRONA TUNC ACCEDEBAT,
ET LUMEN IN FUMUM, ET FUMUM IN LUMEN, ET CONTRA, CONVERTEBAT.

My Lady and her Mayd, upon a merry pin,
They made a match at farting, who should the wager win.
Joan lights three candles then, and sets them bolt upright.
With the first fart she blew them out, with the next she gave them light.
In comes my Lady then, with all her might and maine,
And blew them out, and in, and out, and in, and out again.

William Ellis of Oxford, 1652
Provided by B.W. Robinson

A Graffito for a Pompeian Latrine

IAM SEDEO HIC ANIMUM FRACTUSQUE UT FATA DEPLORO:
ASSE DATO POSSUM NUNC MODO PEDERE EGO.
Here I sit broken-hearted:
Paid a penny and only farted.

FOOD AND DRINK

Every man with a belly full of the classics is an
enemy of the human race.

Henry Miller, American novelist, 1891–1980

MULTOS SOLEBAT SEDULUS IMPROBO
GLUTIRE LURCO MORE CUNICULOS.
TER SORPSIT, HEU! SENOS: RELINQUIT
LURIDUS ET VOMITURUS USUM.

Translated by Tim Ades

There was an old person whose habits
Induced him to feed upon rabbits;
When he'd eaten eighteen,
He turned perfectly green,
Upon which he relinquished those habits.

Edward Lear, English writer, 1812–88

CIBUS   POTUSQUE

FOOD FOR THOUGHT

NON UT VIVAM EDO, UT EDAM VIVO.
I don't eat to live, I live to eat.

FAMES EST OPTIMUS COQUUS.
Hunger is the best cook.

MAGISTER ARTIS INGENIIQUE LARGITOR VENTER.
The stomach is the teacher of the arts and the dispenser of invention.
Persius, *Satires*, Prologue

A Roman Recipe

PHOENICOPTERUM ELIBERAS, LAVAS, ORNAS, INCLUDIS IN CACCABUM; ADICIES AQUAM, SALEM, ANETHUM ET ACETI MODICUM ... AMULO OBLIGAS, IUS PERFUNDUS ET INFERES. IDEM FACIES ET IN PSITTACO.

Pluck the flamingo, wash, truss and put it in a saucepan; add water, salt, dill and a little vinegar ... thicken with cornflour, pour the sauce over the bird and serve. The same method can also be used for parrot.
Apicius, *The Art of Cooking*

CARISSIME, TUA CENA EST IN CANE!
Darling, your dinner is in the dog!
Provided by J.F. Hudson

THE KINDEST CUTS

Useful tips for the Butcher's Shop

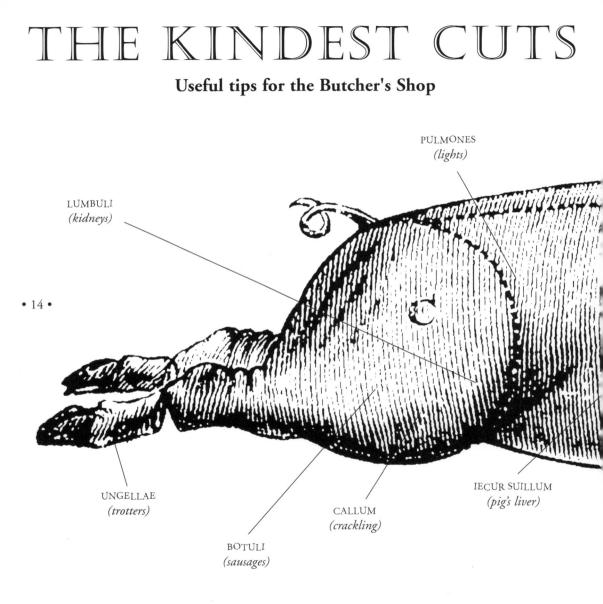

PULMONES
(lights)

LUMBULI
(kidneys)

IECUR SUILLUM
(pig's liver)

UNGELLAE
(trotters)

CALLUM
(crackling)

BOTULI
(sausages)

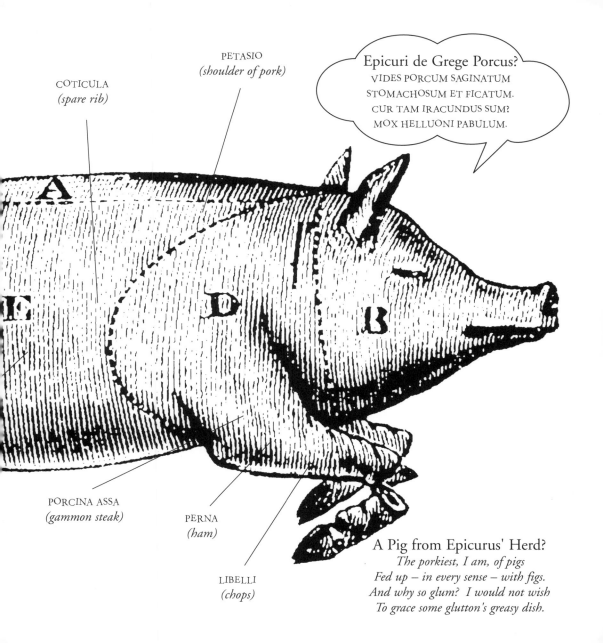

A Pig from Epicurus' Herd?
The porkiest, I am, of pigs
Fed up – in every sense – with figs.
And why so glum? I would not wish
To grace some glutton's greasy dish.

DELICIOUS HOWLERS

More from those schoolboys.
The correct translations are in brackets.

e.g.   *Egg sample*   *(By way of example)*

SARDI VENALES   *Sardines for sale*   *(The easily bribed citizens of Sardinia)*

COCTILIBUS MURIS   *Cocktailed mice*   *(With walls made of burnt brick)*

The ancient Romans were so glutinous that they took emetics in the middle of dinner.

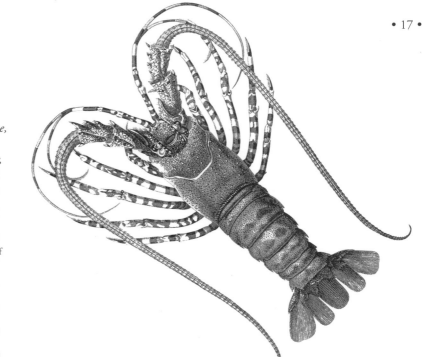

ABIIT,
EXCESSIT,
EVASIT,
ERUPIT.
He went out to dine,
ate too much,
blamed the lobster,
was violently sick.
(He departed,
he withdrew,
he strode off,
he broke forth.)
Provided by W.G. Hoff

IN VINO –
VERITABLE DISASTER!

Latin is a bibulous language.
Here are some useful phrases for the wine bar
and public house.

Wine Sayings:

NUNC EST BIBENDUM.
Now is the time to drink.

EDE, BIBE, ESTO LAETUS, NAM CRAS MORIEMUR.
Eat, drink and be merry for tomorrow we die.

USQUE AD MORTEM BIBENDUM.
Drink till you drop.

MEUM EST PROPOSITUM IN TABERNA MORI.
I intend to spend my last days in a pub.

DELIRIUM TREMENS.
A brain disorder brought on by excessive consumption of alcohol.

IN VINO
VERA CALAMITAS

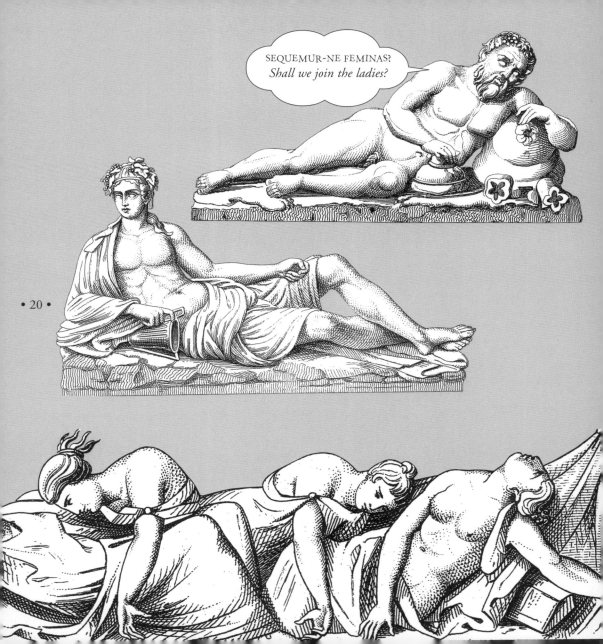

• 20 •

WINE HOWLERS

MULTA SUNT INTER CALICEM ET LABRUM SUMMUM.
There's many a slip 'twixt cup and lip!
See correct translations in brackets.

INTER ALIA	*Something in the ale*	*(Amongst other matters)*
PRO BONO PUBLICO	*To oblige the publican*	*(For the good of the public)*
SOTTO VOCE	*In a drunken voice*	*(Italian: with a soft voice)*

NEC HAUSTA MERI, SED DATA FRUSTRA BIBUNT
Not draughts of wine, but they in vain are drinking dates.
(...and [cups] not drained of unmixed wine, but they are drinking what they have been given in vain.)

WINE SONGS

EBRIO QUID FACIAMUS NAUTA?
What shall we do with a drunken sailor?

HA, HA, HA, URCEOLE! ME DELECTAS MAXIME!
Ha, ha, ha, hee, hee, hee! Little Brown Jug, don't I love thee!

AD ME SI BIBIS OCULIS TUIS...
Drink to me only with thine eyes...

Grace under fire...

BENEDICTUS BENEDICAT.
May the Blessed One bless (this food).

BENEDICTO BENEDICATUR.
May the Blessed One be blessed (in thanksgiving).

BUT ... BENEDICTINE BENE DECANTER.
Maliciously attributed to the Order of St. Benedict.
Provided by W.G. Hoff

HOME SWEET HOME

They were a tense and peculiar
family, the Oedipuses, weren't they?

Max Beerbohm, English writer,
1872–1956

UXORIUS
A hen-pecked husband
Virgil, *Aeneid*, IV

PICA PULVINARIS
Hen-pecker (lit. magpie of the sofa)
Petronius, *Satyricon*

DULCIS DOMUM

Some Family Howlers
The correct translations are in brackets.

STULTISSIMUS SEMPER SUA LAUDAT.
A very foolish man always praises his own wife.
(It is a very foolish man who always praises his own deeds.)

NEMO MORTALIS SAPIET OMNIBUS HORIS.
No mortal man is safe in a public vehicle with a woman.
(No mortal will be sensible at all hours.)

INTER FERIAS COMMENTARIOS MEAS DE VITA MEA SCRIPTITO.
Among the wild beasts I write about my wife.
(I often write about my life in my holiday memoirs.)

• 23 •

MEA MATER MALA SUIS EST.
My mother is a bad pig.
(My mother is unkind to her family.)

PATER CUM PAUCIS ALIIS
The father with the other pigs...
(Father with a few other men...)

MAGNOPERE
Grandfather
(Very much)

HOME TRUTHS

PATER ROMA REGRESSUS MIHI HANC
PEDICULOSAM TOGULAM ATTULIT!
*My father went to Rome and all I got
was this lousy toga!*

DULCE EST DESIPERE IN LOCO.
It is comforting to let oneself go now and again.
Horace, *Odes*, IV.12

QUOD NON FRACTUM EST, NOLI FIGERE.
If it ain't broke, don't fix it!
Provided by Quintin V.S. Bach

DOMUS IN PRATO
Home on the range

FLAMMA FUMO EST PROXIMA.
There's no smoke without fire.

DE FUMO IN FLAMMAS
Out of the frying pan into the fire (lit. out of the smoke into the fire)

PROXIMUS SUM EGOMET MIHI.
Charity begins at home.
Terence, *The Lady of Andros*, 635

DUMQUE MEAE HUIC UXORI MODO BULGA SIT AURI,
FLOCCI PENDO SI BULGA ETIAM SIT ANUS.
*If my wife has a bag of gold,
Do I care if the bag is old?*
Cole Porter, American composer, 1891–1964, *Kiss me, Kate*

VITA EST CANIS ... DEINDE EANDEM DUCIS!
Life's a bitch ... and then you marry one!

DOMESTICA VERA

HOUSEHOLD HINTS

EST RIMA IN HAMA, CARA LISA, CARA LISA.
EST RIMA IN HAMA, CARA LISA, RIMA!
There's a hole in my bucket, dear Liza, dear Liza!
There's a hole in my bucket, dear Liza, a hole.

QUAM CLAUDE, CARE MARCE.	*Then mend it, dear Marcus!*
QUA RE EAM CLAUDO, CARA LISA?	*With what should I mend it, dear Liza?*
STRAMENTO, CARE MARCE.	*With straw, dear Marcus!*
EST NIMIUM LONGUM, CARA LISA.	*The straw is too long, dear Liza!*
DECIDE STRAMENTUM, CARE MARCE.	*Then cut it, dear Marcus!*
QUO MODO DECIDO, CARA LISA?	*With what should I cut it, dear Liza?*
SECURI, CARE MARCE.	*With an axe, dear Marcus!*
SECURIS EST HEBES, CARA LISA.	*The axe is blunt, dear Liza!*
ACUE SECURIM, CARE MARCE.	*Then sharpen it, dear Marcus!*
QUO MODO ACUO, CARA LISA?	*With what should I sharpen it, dear Liza?*
QUAM COTE ACUE, CARE MARCE.	*With a whet-stone, dear Marcus!*
EST COS NIMIS SICCA, CARA LISA.	*The whet-stone's too dry, dear Liza!*
QUAM MADEFAC COTEM, CARE MARCE	*Then wet it, dear Marcus!*
QUO MODO MADEFACIO, CARA LISA?	*With what should I wet it, dear Liza?*
FER AQUAM, CARE MARCE.	*Fetch water, dear Marcus!*
QUO MODO FERO AQUAM, CARA LISA?	*Then how should I fetch it, dear Liza?*
IN HAMA, CARE MARCE.	*In a bucket, dear Marcus!*
EST RIMA IN HAMA, CARA LISA.	*There's a hole in my bucket, dear Liza!*

LOVE AND LUST

Naturally, the first of the red hot lovers were Latin.
Here are some useful lines for the bar
and bedroom, and everywhere
along the way.

HABITABAT PUELLA NAUPACTI
CRUCIATA CUPIDINE CACTI,
DOLIS BENE FUNCTA
SPINIS MALE PUNCTA:
CACTO RESTAT NOMEN INTACTI.

There was a young girl from Naupactus
Who had an affair with a cactus.
Though she tried many tricks
And endured many pricks,
Still the cactus is virgo intactus.
Limerick and translation by Jasper Griffin

VENERES LIBIDINESQUE

USEFUL CHAT-UP LINES

Literary

NUM LICET AESTIVO MIHI TE CONFERRE DIEI?

Shall I compare thee to a summer's day?

William Shakespeare, English dramatist and poet, 1564–1616, *Sonnets*, 18
Translated by Rev. A.H. Wratislaw

HORTUM, LYDIA, IAM PETAS!

Come into the garden, Maud!

Alfred, Lord Tennyson, English poet, 1809–92, *Maud*, I.22
Translated by Rev. J.S. Purton

Tried and Tested

SALVE, NAUTA!

Hello, sailor!

FREQUENTASNE HUNC LOCUM?

Do you come here often?

SI DICAM CORPUS FORMOSUM TIBI ESSE, TU ID HABEAS ADVERSUS ME?

If I said you had a beautiful body, would you hold it against me?

PRAEBES SPECIEM GELIDAM, SED SUBTER ES IPSE VESUVIUS: SIC ARBITROR.

You look cool but I bet you're Vesuvius underneath.

SPHINGULA!

You little sphinx!

RESTAT MIHI MODO SPATIUM SEPTEM DIERUM AD VIVENDUM.

I have only one week to live.

Classic

QUID IUDICAS DE CATULLO LESBIAQUE? CENSES EOS CONCILIATIONEM FACTUROS ESSE?

What's your feeling about Catullus and Lesbia? Do you think they could work it out?

MIHI EST COLLATIO NON EXPURGATA EPIGRAMMATON MARTIALIS APUD ME. VIS-NE EAM VIDERE?

I've got an unexpurgated set of Martial's epigrams at my house. Would you like to see it?

QUEM LOCUM TENES DE VERSU PENTAMETRO IAMBICO? MAVIS-NE VERSUM HEXAMETRUM
DACTYLICUM? RECTE DICIS: SIC EST RHYTHMUS MAGIS LIBIDINOSUS.

What's your position on iambic pentameter? You prefer dactylic hexameter? Me too: the rhythm is sexier.

PUT DOWNS

SUNT MIHI CAPILLI FLUENTES, FUSCI OCULI, CORPUS COLORATUM.
QUID, SI VIS, EST MEA PROPRIETAS OPTIMA?
I have flowing locks, dark brown eyes, a sun-tanned body.
What, would you say, is my best feature?

SINE DUBIO, EST TUA VILLA IN ETRURIA.
Definitely your villa in Tuscany.

CREDO ME POSSE TE MAXIME DELECTARE.
I believe I can give you the greatest pleasure.

QUID ENIM? TU-NE DISCEDES?
Why? Are you leaving?

NONNE PRIMUS SUM QUI TEMPTAVI TE
CORRUMPERE?
I'm the first man who has ever tried to
seduce you, aren't I?

FORTASSE: FACIES TUA
MIHI NOTA VIDETUR.
You could be: your face
looks familiar.

UT ALIQUANDO MECUM CENES ORO.
I beg you, have dinner with me some time!

UT POSSIM, METUO: DOLOREM CAPITIS ILLO DIE FERAM.
I'm afraid I can't: I'm having a headache on that day.

NONNE ANTEA TIBI ALICUBI OCCURRI?
Haven't I met you somewhere before?

VERISIMILE EST: SUM AMICA TUAE FILIAE.
Probably: I'm a friend of your daughter's.

EST-NE PUGIO IN TOGA ...
VEL SOLUM TIBI LIBET ME VIDERE?
Is that a dagger in your toga ... or are you
just pleased to see me?

MINIME ... EST PUGIO.
No ... it's a dagger.

LIBET-NE ALIQUID TOMACULI
FERVENTIS ETIAM SUMERE?
Have you still got room for
a hot sausage?

CARO PUTRIDA ES,
OLENS ALIUM!
You're dead meat,
garlic breath!

PERSONAL ADS

QUADRAGINTA ANNOS NATUS VETERANUS MILES IN PUNICIS BELLIS, HABENS MAGNUM PILUM LEVITER CORROSUMQUE CICATRICOSUMQUE, QUAERIT COMEM COTEM QUI ASPERAS ACIES LEVIGET.

capsa XIV

40-year-old veteran of the Punic Wars, with large slightly serrated and scarred javelin, seeks friendly whet-stone to smooth off rough edges.

Box 14

SOLITARIA COLUMNA DORICA EGET GRATO ATRIO.

capsa XLIII

Lonely doric column is in need of pleasant atrium.

Box 43

LICET VERBO 'UT' MODO SUBJUNCTIVO UTI; LICENTIA AUTEM MIHI EST. LIBET-NE TIBI ANOMALIS VERBIS UTI?

capsa LXIX

'ut' takes the subjunctive; I take liberties. Are you into irregular verbs?

Box 69

DOMINA INSIGNIS BREVITATE FUSCOQUE COLORE, QUAE VILLAM IN VIA APPIA POSSIDET, EXQUIRIT HOMINEM MINIMUM ORDINIS SENATORII ORNATUMQUE SUA DOMO IN URBE, DOMINUMQUE MINIMUM SEXAGINTA DOMESTICORUM SERVORUM.

capsa XCIV

Petite dark lady, own villa on the Appian Way, seeks man of at least senator status with own house in town and a minimum of sixty indoor slaves.

Box 94

VIR, VALENS, DIVES, CUI SUI SUNT DENTES, PETIT VIRGINEM VESTALEM CORRUMPENDAM VIOLANDAMQUE.

capsa CXV

Man, virile, rich, own teeth, seeks Vestal Virgin for corruption and desecration.

Box 115

AENEAE EXEMPLAR CUPIT DIDONIS EXEMPLAR QUOD LUDAT.

capsa CXXXVII

Aeneas-type desires Dido-type for dalliance.

Box 137

A LATIN PASSION PRIMER

How to get from foreplay to afterglow in eleven easy steps

SECUNDAM-NE MENSAM PRAETERMITTEMUS?
Shall we skip dessert?

LABAR MODO IN VESTEM COMMODIOREM.
*I'll just slip into something more
comfortable.*

NONNE NIMIS CALES IN ILLA?
Aren't you dreadfully hot in that?

FIT MELIUS.
That's better.

AMPLECTERE ME.
Hold me!

DA MIHI OSCULA.
Kiss me!

AD INFERNA.
Lower!

SIC, ISTIC!
Yes, there!

O VENUS! O IUPPITER!
Oh, Venus! Oh, Jupiter!

TE AMO.
I love you.

MINIME. NON ITA OMNIBUS
PUELLIS/PUERIS DICTITO.
No. I don't say that to all the girls/boys.

How to seduce, pleasure and titillate in *Classical* Latin

Some lines from the old master, Ovid, author of *Ars Amatoria, The Art of Loving*

UT LOQUERER TECUM VENI, TECUMQUE SEDEREM NE TIBI NON NOTUS, QUEM FACIS, ESSET AMOR.
Amores III.2
I have come to talk with you, to sit with you to make sure you realise the passion you are arousing in me.

NULLI TUA FORMA SECUNDA EST.
Amores I.8
Your beauty is second to none.

MEA LUX
Amores I.4
Light of my life!

VIX A TE VIDEOR POSSE TENERE MANUS.
Amores I.4
I can scarcely keep my hands off you.

SPECTA ME ... VERBA SUPERCILIIS SINE VOCE LOQUENTIA DICAM.
Amores I.4
Look at me ... I shall speak to you with the voiceless language of my eyebrows.

QUA TU BIBERIS, HAC EGO PARTE BIBAM.
Amores I.4
Where you have touched the cup's brim with your lips, I'll kiss.

QUANTUM ET QUALE LATUS! QUAM IUVENALE FEMUR!
Amores I.5
What a svelte and willowy form! You have the slender thighs of a girl!

PRETIUM MIHI DULCE REPENDE CONCUBITUS HODIE ... TUOS.
Amores II.8
Today I'm holding you to ransom and you must pay me back with kisses and caresses!

EXCIPIAMQUE UMERIS ET MULTA SINE ORDINE CARPAM OSCULA.
Amores II.11
And I shall take you in my arms and wildly cover you with kisses galore.

TECUM, QUOS DEERINT ANNOS MIHI FILA SORORUM VIVERE CONTINGAT.
Amores I.3
May it be my destiny to live with you the years which the Sister Fates' threads have spun for me!

LOVE CONQUERS ALL

VAE VOBIS, LIBYCUM PECUS, CAMELI! SPHINGA
VERE NOVO LIBIDINOSI PERVERSE PENETRARE DESTINATIS,
CUIUS POSTERIORA, NE PETANTUR, OBSTRUCTAE BENE PROTEGUNT HARENAE.
HINC VOBIS TUMOR ISTE. TU TAMEN, SPHINX, SEMPER IMPENETRABILIS RENIDES.
Translated by Mark Mortimer

The sexual life of the camel is odder than anyone thinks:
At the height of the mating season, he attempts to ravish the sphinx.
But the nether parts of the sphinx are clogged by the sands of the Nile,
Which accounts for the hump of the camel and the sphinx's inscrutable smile!
Traditional

OMNIA VINCIT AMOR ... PRAETER PAUPERTATEM
Love conquers everything ... except poverty

OMNIA VINCIT AMOR

Virgil, *Eclogues*, X

DOLOREMQUE DENTIS.
and toothache.

Mac West, American actress, 1892–1980

Pathetic Phall-acy
POST COITUM OMNE ANIMAL TRISTE.
After coition every animal is sad.
Anonymous Latin saying

LOVE HURTS

ALIQUID PECTORA TENET.
Something's gotten hold of my heart.

SUB CUTE TE HABEO.
I've got you under my skin.

SOLUS ES QUEM VELIM ... A, A, A, MEL!
You're the one that I want ... ooh, ooh, ooh, honey!

COMMOVES ANIMUM ... DULCIFER.
I've got a crush on you ... sweetie-pie.

MIHI FERTUR ESSE ALIQUID BONI.
Something tells me I'm into something good.

UNA SUMUS FORMOSI.
Together we are beautiful.

SEMPER TE AMABO.
I will always love you.

QUAE FACTA SUNT A ME OMNIA OB TE.
Everything I do, I do it for you.

SONGS

NOCET AMOR

AMISSA TUA CURA.
You've lost that loving feeling.

NON IAM COLLOQUIMUR.
We don't talk any more.

NUM CUPIS ME, CARA?
Don't you want me, baby?

SI ME DESERIS, ADIMIS MAXIMAM PARTEM MEI.
If you leave me now, you take away the biggest part of me.

FULGEBIT SOL NON IAM POSTEA.
The sun ain't gonna shine any more.

UBINAM SUNT FLORES, DIC.
Where have all the flowers gone?

SOLUMQUE SOLI...
Only the lonely...

NOLO ID COMMEMORARE.
I don't want to talk about it.

SUPERERO.
I will survive.

SUNG BLUE IN LATIN

LOVE AND DEATH

A tale of illicit passion, jealousy and revenge ...
... or how Hollywood might adapt *The Shorter Latin Primer*?

Scene: Sitting room of the Hillards' home. Mrs. Hillard is knitting. Enter Mr. North.
Mr. North (holding out his hands): AMO!
Mrs. Hillard (surprised but pleased): AMAS? *(to herself):* AMAT!
Both (reaching out and taking hold of one another's hands): AMAMUS.
Enter Mr. Hillard.
Mr. Hillard (angrily): AMATIS? *(looks heavenward)* AMANT!
(He pulls out a gun): NECABO.
Mr. North (horrorstruck): NECABIS?
Mrs. Hillard (wails): NECABIT!
Enter Mrs. North holding rifle.

Mrs. North and Mr. Hillard (together): NECABIMUS.
Mr. North: NECABITIS?
Mr. North and Mrs. Hillard (retreating together): NECABUNT!
Mr. Hillard shoots Mr. North who falls to the ground.
Mr. North: MORTUUS SUM.
Mrs. Hillard: NON MORTUUS ES.
Mr. Hillard: MORTUUS EST.
Mrs. North shoots Mrs. Hillard.
Mrs. Hillard and Mr. North (together): MORTUI SUMUS.
They die.
Mrs. North and Mr. Hillard (together): MORTUI ESTIS?
They look at each other in satisfaction.
Both: MORTUI SUNT.
exeunt, arm in arm.
Written by Margaret Rowley

Useful glossary:— AMO ... *I love;* NECABO ... *I shall kill;* MORTUUS SUM ... *I am dead*

AMOR MORSQUE

QUIPPE MINUTI SEMPER ET INFIRMI EST ANIMI EXIGUIQUE VOLUPTAS ULTIO. CONTINUO SIC COLLIGE,
QUOD VINDICATA NEMO MAGIS GAUDET QUAM FEMINA.

*For revenge is always the delight of a mean spirit, of a weak and petty mind. You may immediately draw
proof of this — that no-one rejoices more in revenge than a woman.*
Juvenal, *Satires*, XIII

DIS MANIBVS
C . LICINI C . LIB .
PRIMIGENI ET
LICINIAE C . LIB .
HYGIAE

Love Howlers

*There is also the hidden sexual innuendo (inutile ferrum)
that [Priam's] age has caused him to reach
sexual impudence.*
Provided by Lynda Goss

The emblem of Dionysus was a huge callus.
Provided by Matthew Macleod

LXXX
love and kisses

DOGS AND DOGGEREL

SIMIA QUAM SIMILIS, TURPISSIMA BESTIA, NOBIS!
The ape, vilest of beasts, how like to us!
Cicero (quoting Ennius), *On the Nature of the Gods*, I.35

PUELLA RIGENSIS RIDEBAT
QUAM TIGRIS IN TERGO VEHEBAT;
EXTERNA PROFECTA
INTERNA REVECTA
SED RISUS CUM TIGRIS MANEBAT.
Anonymous, 1854

There was a young lady of Riga
Who went for a ride on a tiger;
They returned from the ride
With the lady inside
And a smile on the face of the tiger.
Traditional

CANES CARMINAQUE INCULTA

BESTIAL LATIN

Some Animal Howlers
The correct translations are in brackets.

GALLI CONCLAMABANT QUOD GERMANOS SUB IUGUM DEIECERUNT.
The cocks were crowing because they had laid a German egg.
(The Gauls were shouting loudly because they subjugated the Germans.)

VERE NOVO GELIDUS CANIS CUM MONTIBUS HUMOR LIQUITUR.
Startling but true the cold hound was left on the mountains by way of a joke.
(At the beginning of spring when icy streams trickle from the snowy mountains...)
Provided by W.G. Hoff

APES MEL COMPARABANT.
The apes were preparing a meal.
(Bees provided honey.)

AVES ALTA PETUNT.
The birds are getting high.
(The birds make for the heights.)

AVE, DOMINE.
Lord, I am a bird.
(Hail, Lord!)

DIDO ET DUX
Dido ate ducks.
(Dido and the commander)

FELICES AMBO
I shall love cats.
(Both fortunate)

POST EQUITEM SEDET ATRA
CURA.
After horse exercise the black lady
sits down with care.
(Black anxiety sits behind the
cavalryman.)

CORNIGERI BOVES
Corned beef
(Horned cattle)

And an Ancient Howler
Bears when first born are shapeless masses of white flesh a little larger than mice, their claws
alone being prominent. The mother then licks them gradually into proper shape.
Pliny the Elder, *Natural History*, VIII

UT CAUDAM CROCODILUS, ECCE, PARVUS
CURAT CONTINUO SUAM NITENTEM;
LYMPHA NILIACA IRRIGAT LAVATQUE
SQUAMAS SEGNITER AUREAS ADUSQUE!
QUAM RICTUS HILARES FREQUENTER EDIT!
UNGUES ORDINE CALLIDE PANDIT;
MALIS PISCICULOS CAPIT BENIGNE
SUBRIDENTIBUS, HOSCE PELLICITQUE.

Translated by Clive Harcourt Carruthers,
from *Alicia in Terra Mirabili*

How doth the little crocodile
Improve his shining tail,
And pour the waters of the Nile
On every golden scale!
How cheerfully he seems to grin,
How neatly spread his claws,
And welcome little fishes in
With gently smiling jaws!

Lewis Carroll (Charles Dodgson), English writer,
1832–98, from *Alice in Wonderland*

• 40 •

The Birth of an Ancient Aphorism

It has been related that dogs drink at the river Nile running
along, that they may not be seized by the crocodiles.

Phaedrus, *Fables*, I.25

"To treat a thing as dogs do the Nile" was, in ancient times,
a common way of describing superficial attention.

CATULUS NON MODO IN DIES
FESTOS SED ETIAM IN VITAM EST!
*A puppy is for life ...
not just for Christmas!*

• 41 •

MICA, VESPERTILIO!
QUIDNAM AGAS DUBITO!
SUPRA MUNDUM VOLITAS,
FERCULUMQUE SIMULAS.

Translated by Clive Harcourt Carruthers,
from *Alicia in Terra Mirabili*

Twinkle, twinkle, little bat!
How I wonder what you're at!
Up above the world you fly,
Like a tea-tray in the sky.

Lewis Carroll (Charles Dodgson), English writer,
1832–98, from *Alice in Wonderland*

TRES MURES, TRES MURES
CAECI CURRUNT, EN FUGIUNT!
SEQUUNTUR AGRICOLAE UXOREM,
QUAE CAUDAS EXSECUIT CULTRO. REM
CONSPEXISTI TU TAM MIRABILEM
QUAM TRES MURES?!

Three Blind Mice, three blind mice,
See how they run, see how they run!
They all ran after the farmer's wife,
Who cut off their tails with a carving knife.
Did you ever see such a thing in your life
As three blind mice?

Traditional

A NURSERY BESTIARY

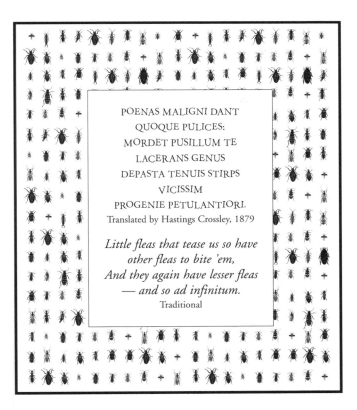

POENAS MALIGNI DANT
QUOQUE PULICES:
MORDET PUSILLUM TE
LACERANS GENUS
DEPASTA TENUIS STIRPS
VICISSIM
PROGENIE PETULANTIORI.

Translated by Hastings Crossley, 1879

Little fleas that tease us so have
other fleas to bite 'em,
And they again have lesser fleas
— and so ad infinitum.

Traditional

AGNELLUS MARIAE ERAT.
A PATRE INTERFECTUS
AD LUDUM NUNC ADSEQUITUR
IN PANIBUS PORRECTUS.

Mary had a little lamb.
Her father killed it dead.
So now it follows her to school
Between two slabs of bread.

Traditional

SPORT — THE BEAUTIFUL GAMES

Saturday afternoon at the Colosseum. The goalposts
haven't moved very far in two thousand years.

NIMIUM VAGA TURBA
The fiendishly fickle mob
Ovid, *Amores*, II.9

QUI UNUM CERTAMEN LETIFERUM ASPEXIT, OMNIA VIDIT.
Seen one fight to the death, seen 'em all.

VOX ET PRAETEREA NIHIL
All talk and no action

NIL ILLEGITIMI CARBORUNDUM!
Don't let the bastards get you down!
Provided by W.G. Hoff

VICTOR OMNIA ACCIPIT.
Winner takes all.

OPINOR VENTUM ESSE IN TEMPORIS SPATIUM ADDITUM VULNERATIS.
I think they're into injury time.

PUTANT ACTUM ESSE ... RE VERA NUNC!
They think it's all over ... it is now!

LUDI VENUSTI

HOW TO GET AHEAD IN BUSINESS

REM FACIAS, REM SI POSSIS RECTE,
SI NON, QUOCUMQUE MODO REM.
*Make money, money by fair means if you
can; if not, by any means money.*
Horace, *Epistles*, I.1

AURA SACRA FAMES!
O accurst craving for gold!
Virgil, *Aeneid*, III

NIL POSSE CREARI DE NILO.
Nothing can be created from nothing.
Lucretius, *On the Nature of Things*, I

HIC VIVIMUS AMBITIOSA PAUPERTATE OMNES.
We all live in a state of ambitious poverty.
Juvenal, *Satires*, III

CUI BONO?
To whose advantage?
Cicero, *Pro Milone*, XII

ARS SUPERANDI IN NEGOTIO

Useful Phrases

NUMMI, NUMMI, NUMMI ... EN MUNDUS DIVITIS!
Money, money, money ... it's a rich man's world!

ACUMEN MIHI, VENUSTAS TIBI — QUAESTUM APPETAMUS!
I've got the brains, you've got the looks — let's make lots of money!

QUIS VULT FIERI PRAEDIVES? EGOMET.
Who wants to be a millionaire? I do.

INTENTIO ADMINISTRATORIS
Executive Stress

VIA MOENIUM	PROPOLA PERNIX	SAGINAE
Wall Street	*Wheeler Dealer*	*Fat Cats*

NEQUE PROTINUS
UNO EST CONDITA ROMA DIE.
Rome was not built in a day.
Pietro Angelo Manzolli, Sixteenth-Century
Latin poet, *Zodiacus Vitae*

Desktop Latin

VIDISTI-NE NOSTRAM PAGINAM DOMESTICAM?
Have you seen our Home Page?

TRANSCURRENS RETICULUM
Surfing the Net

INSTRUCTUS
Online

GESTAMEN STABILE
Hard drive

FLEXIBILES ORBICULI
Floppy disks

CIMEX MILLE ANNORUM
Millennium bug

COMPUTATOR GESTABILIS IN GREMIO
Laptop

TABULA
Keyboard

LIBELLUS ELECTRONICUS QUI
COMPUTATOREM REGIT
Programme

HABES EPISTULAS.
You've got mail.

RES FERME VERA
Virtual Reality

MACHINA QUAE EPISTULAS PER AETHERA
TRANSMITTIT
Fax

Your Mobile Phone

HEUS ... SALVE ...
Hello ... Hello ...

POTES-NE ME AUDIRE?
Can you hear me?

TUA VOX QUASI FLUCTUANS ...
You're coming and going ...

ADHUC ILLIS STAS?
Are you still there?

PILA ELECTRICA DEFICIT.
My battery is running low.

EST CONTURBATIO ...
There's interference ...

HIC SERMO MIHI CONSTAT PECUNIA MULTA.
This conversation is costing me a fortune!

IN TEMPORE SOLITO DOMUM ADVENIAM.
I'll be home at the usual time.

QUID MIHI DABIS EDENDO?
What's for dinner?

MOTTOES AND SLOGANS

For the House of Commons or Congress:

AUT TACE AUT LOQUERE MELIORA SILENTIO.
Either be silent or say something superior to silence.

For a Manufacturer of Paint:

O TEMPURA, O MUROS!
O — for tempera and walls!
(After Cicero's "O tempora, o mores"
O — for my times and for morality!)
Provided by Jackie Murphy

For a Golf Club:

AB UNO ICTU
A hole in one

For a Used Car Dealer:

NULLUM TAURI EXCRETUM
No bullshit

For a Car Wash:

AQUA VALET.
Water has power.
(But also includes the English meaning of valet and a pun on ave atque vale! Hail and farewell!)
Provided by Quintin V.S. Bach

For a School:

DISCE AUT DISCEDE.
Learn or leave!

Multi-purpose Mottoes

PRAEMONITUS PRAEMUNITUS
Forewarned is forearmed.

SEMPER PARATUS OR NUNQUAM NON PARATUS
Ever ready

UBIQUE
Any time, any place, anywhere

SEMPER PARATUS

WHEN IN ROME...

SI FUERIS ROMAE, ROMANO VIVITO MORE ...
...SI FUERIS ALIBI, VIVITO SICUT IBI.

When in Rome, live like the Romans ...
... when elsewhere, live as they do there!

TU, BRITANNIA, HERA PRAESIS MARI
BRITANNI VERE NUMQUAM SINT SERVI

Rule Britannia, Britannia rules the waves
Britons never, never, never shall be slaves.

CULTA BRITANNIA

"Cool Britannia"

REGINA, PER DEUM,
PRAECLARA NOBILUM,
DIU VIVAT!

God save our gracious Queen,
Long live our noble Queen,
God save our Queen!

PUER IANCHIUS SUM SPLENDENS
QUI SIT FACERE AUT MORI!
IN DIE LIBERTATIS NATUS,
NEPOS SUM SAM AVUNCULI!

I'm a Yankee Doodle Dandy
Yankee Doodle do or die!
A real life nephew of my Uncle Sam
Born on the Fourth of July!

O DIC NUM DESPECTET STELLANS
VEXILLUM
LIBERAM PATRIAM FORTIUMQUE
DOMUM.

O say does the star spangled banner
still wave
O'er the land of the free and the home
of the brave?

When in Rome Howlers

Why did the Romans build
straight roads?

(1) ... so that the Britons could not hide
round the corners.

(2) ... for their enemies to run down.

Some Sayings

DIVIDE ET IMPERA
divide and rule

NOVUS HOMO
new man

PUBLICE COMMODUM
politically correct (P.C.)

SI FUERIS ROMAE...

STATE of the BRITONS at the time of the ROMAN INVASION.

W.M.Craig del.   I.Neagle Sc.

THE MOST FAMOUS

Julius Caesar, the quintessential Roman dictator, inspired some of the greatest literature — the worst puns and howlers — in any language, ancient or modern.

Caesar on Caesar

I came, I saw, I conquered
VENI, VIDI, VICI

On his incontinence when
confronted by Asterix and co:
VENI, VIDI ... VIVI!
(wee-wee)

On observing the enemy drinking a magic potion:
VENI, VIDI ... VISCI!
(whisky)

... on second thoughts ... just a small one:
... TINI VINI
(teeny-weeny)

On his subsequent career as a trick cyclist:
VENI, VIDI ... VILI!
(wheelie)

On the British climate's sending him
down with pneumonia:
VENI, VIDI ... VIZI!
(wheezy)

On his experience of the brothels of Pompeii:
VENI, VICI ... V.D.
Provided by Alec Taylor and W.G. Hoff

On his one-time political opponent (after Gertrude Stein):
CICERO CICERO CICERO
(A rose is a rose is a rose)
Provided by David Harvey

NOTISSIMUS

Some Caesar Howlers

Julius Caesar entered Rome wearing a coral reef.
Cassius accused Brutus of taking bribes from the sardines.
Anthony offered Caesar a cornet but he had other ambitions.

Some "pig" Latin

CAESAR ADSUM JAM FORTE
Caesar had some jam for tea.

BRUTUS ADERAT
Brutus had a rat.

CAESAR SIC IN OMNIBUS
Caesar sick in omnibus.

BRUTUS SIC IN AT`
Brutus sick in hat.
Provided by W.G. Hoff

• 53 •

CAESAR CARI DONA MILITARI ORGI VERSUS
Caesar carried on a military orgy versus

BELGAE, HELVETII, GERMANI, VENETII,
Belgae, Helvetii, Germani, Venetii,

BRITANNI IUNEMIT
Britanni – you name it.

"ROMIS GLORIUS," SED CAESAR,
"Rome is glorious," said Caesar,

"NOMEN ME IMPUNIT!"
"No men may impugn it!"

MENI TRIDIT VERCINGETORIX FORIN STANS.
Many tried it – Vercingetorix, for instance.

CAESAR NOCTEM SILI FORS TICINIS NEC AUT.
Caesar knocked him silly for sticking his neck out.

AB LUDI NERVI FELO, CAIUS IULIUS, IUBET.
A bloody nervy fellow, Gaius Julius, you bet.
Traditional – one of several versions in circulation

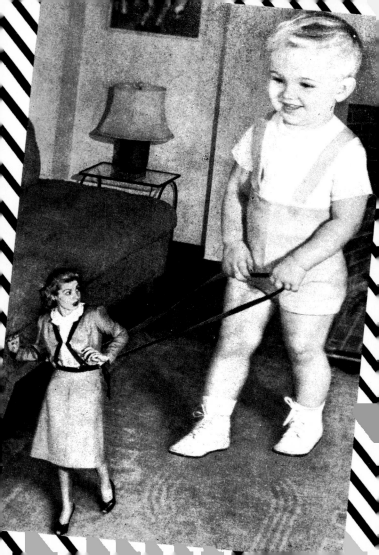

CRUELTY TO THE CLASSICS

A little learning is a dangerous thing. As usual, the correct translations for these howlers are in brackets.

Pompeii was destroyed by an overflow of saliva from the Vatican.

POETA NASCITUR, NON FIT.
Don't blame the poet, he was born like it.
(A poet is born, not made.)

Virgil was in love with a girl called Enid and wrote lots of books about her.

Ovid wrote a poem called the Medea which was lost fortunately.

Gladiators give out a great deal of heat.

A centurion in history was a man who had lived a hundred years or over. They don't have them now.

A senator was half horse half man.

The gorgons looked like women only more horrible.

Cicero was killed by a prescription.

Plato was the god of the underground.

NATE DEA
Swim, goddess!
(son of a goddess)

MALIGNITAS
MAIORIBUS

EVERYONE'S A CRITIC

CONSUETUDO MALI TENET INSANABILE MULTOS SCRIBENDI CACOETHES ET AEGRO IN CORDE SENESCIT.
An inveterate and incurable itch for writing besets many and grows old in their sick hearts.
Juvenal, *Satires*, VI

NIHIL TAM ABSURDUM DICI POTEST UT NON DICATUR A PHILOSOPHO.
There is nothing so ridiculous that it cannot have been said by a philosopher.
Cicero, *On Divination*, II

QUISQUE CRITICUS

MACARONICS

Macaronics are a minestrone of English and Latinate words.
Here are two amusing examples.

Aestivation

In candent ire the solar spendour flames;
The foles, languescent, pend from arid rames;
His humid front the cive, anheling, wipes,
And dreams of erring on ventiferous ripes.

How dulce to vive occult to mortal eyes,
Dorm on the herb with none to supervise,
Carp the suave berries from the crescent vine,
And bibe the flow from longicaudate kine!

To me, alas, no verdurous visions come,
Save yon exiguous pool's convervid scum —
No concave vast repeats the tender hue
That laves my milk jug with celestial blue.

Me wretched! Let me curr to quercine shades!
Effund your albid hausts, lactiferous maids!
O, might I vole to some umbraceous clump,
Depart, be off, excede, evade, erump!

Oliver Wendell Holmes, American writer, 1809–94,
from *The Autocrat of the Breakfast Table*

What is it that roareth thus?
Can it be a motorbus?
Yes, the smell and hideous hum
Indicate motorem bum.

How shall wretches live like us
Cincto bis motoribus?
Domine, defende nos
Contra hos motores bos.

Provided by W.G. Hoff and attributed to Alfred Denis Godley.
This is one of several versions of this macaronic.

...ASSIC MIX AND MATCH

Masculine

EST TIBI... *you have...*

...en just add one word from the adjectives column (1) and one from the nouns (2)

e.g. EST TIBI CONSPICUUS NASUS = *you have a striking nose*
EST TIBI SCABER CANIS = *you have a scabby dog*

1) Adjectives

FOEDUS	*disgusting*
CAPILLATUS	*hairy*
GLABER	*bald*
PARVUS	*small*
STULTUS	*moronic*
RARUS	*rare*
SORDIDUS	*dirty*
BELLUS	*lovely*
LORIPES	*bandy-legged*
HOSTILIS	*aggressive*
LEPIDUS	*charming*
OBLIQUUS	*lop-sided*
CONSPICUUS	*striking*
SCABER	*scabby*

(2) Nouns

CAPILLUS	*head of hair*
VENTER	*belly*
SINUS	*chest*
VERTEX	*head*
RISUS	*smile*
ODORATUS	*smell*
HORTUS	*garden*
RACEMUS NUCUM	*bunch of nuts*
INCESSUS	*walk*
ANIMUS	*spirit*
VICINUS	*neighbour*
NASUS	*nose*
CANIS	*dog*
MODUS VIVENDI	*way of living*

EST TIBI FOEDUS VENTER.

BUILD YOUR OWN INSULTS AND COMPLIMENTS

Feminine

EST TIBI... *you have...*

then just add one word from the adjectives column (1) and one from the nouns (2)

e.g. EST TIBI VENUSTA LOCUTIO = *you have a delightful way of talking*
EST TIBI ARTIFICIOSA CAESARIES = *you have an artificial head of hair*

(1) Adjectives

VENUSTA	*delightful*
ARTIFICIOSA	*artificial*
PERTINAX	*stubborn*
DULCIS	*sweet*
PINGUIS	*plump*
LASCIVA	*playful*
SILA	*snub-nosed*
MAGNA	*big*
EBRIOSA	*drink-loving*
RUGOSA	*wrinkly*
MAMMEATA	*large-breasted*
AGRESTIS	*ill-bred*
TENUIS	*thin*
VACUA	*empty*
PRAVA	*distorted*

(2) Nouns

CERVIX	*neck*
SOCRUS	*mother-in-law*
LABIA	*lip*
VOX	*voice*
MANUS	*hand*
FELES	*cat*
FACIES	*face*
CAESARIES	*head of hair*
PERSONA	*personality*
FRONS	*forehead*
AMICA	*friend*
LOCUTIO	*way of talking*
STOLA	*dress*
RATIO	*bank account*
GENA	*cheek*

• 59 •

EST TIBI DULCIS FRONS.

QUIZ: TEST YOUR LATIN

PER ARDUA AD ASTRA

INFRA DIG means
(1) terrible lodgings;
(2) when someone nudges you;
(3) beneath one's dignity?

SIC TRANSIT means
(1) rough crossing;
(2) the nausea will pass away;
(3) that's how things change?

FLAGRANTE DELICTO means
(1) flagrant delight;
(2) a sweet flavour;
(3) red-handed?

ARIADNE GLADIUM EI DEDIT means
(1) Ariadne gave him the glad eye;
(2) Ariadne dedicated her eyes;
(3) Ariadne gave him a sword?

IN LOCO PARENTIS means
(1) following in father's footsteps;
(2) family sleeping compartment of a train;
(3) in the place of a parent?

AB OVO USQUE AD MALA means
(1) from beginning to end;
(2) it's up to the male to lay eggs?

Answers on

WORDPOWER

DE GUSTIBUS NON EST
DISPUTANDUM means
(1) there's no accounting for tastes;
(2) high winds and no mistake?

NE PLUS ULTRA means
(1) there is nothing beyond Ulster;
(2) perfection?

DUM SPIRO, SPERO means
(1) where there's life, there's hope;
(2) stupid Greek person, I presume?

PER ARDUA AD ASTRA means
(1) through adversity to the stars;
(2) to fall from the stars is hard?

NOTA BENE means
(1) note well;
(2) without any money?

AUT CAESAR AUT NIL means
(1) all or nothing;
(2) an Italian football result?

CAVEAT EMPTOR means
(1) let the buyer beware;
(2) look out, it's empty?

• 61 •

ARIADNE
GLADIUM
EI DEDIT

DEAD AND BURIED

Sometimes unfairly described as a dead language, Latin has a life
of its own when it comes to describing death.

RYDENSIS PUELLA, QUAE EDIT
MALUM IMMATURUM, DECEDIT.
IN VENTRE TURGESCIT;
DEFLETA SPUMESCIT
NEC VINUM DIVINUM IMPEDIT.
Translated by Mary Holtby

There was a young lady of Ryde
Who ate a green apple and died.
The apple fermented
Within the lamented
And made cider inside her inside.
Traditional

Some Death Howlers
The correct translations are in brackets.

A.D.	*After death*	*(anno domini:* *In the year of our Lord)*
in mortuis nil nisi bonum.	*In the dead there's* *nothing but bones.*	*(In the dead there's* *nothing but good.)*
	'habeas corpus' was a *phrase used at the time of* *the great plague and means* *'bring out your dead.'*	*(You may have the body.)*
Crematorium is the Latin form of dairy.		

MORTUUS SEPULTUSQUE

EPITAPHS

IAM CERTE SCIO, SUSPICATUS OLIM,
ID QUOD CUNCTA DOCENT, IOCUM ESSE VITAM.
Translated by J.F. Davies, 1869

Life's a jest; and all things show it.
I thought so once; but now I know it.
John Gay, English poet, 1685–1732, My Own Epitaph

On a Busy Woman

ERGO AGITE, O COMITES,
LACRIMAS MIHI SISTITE INANES,
NAMQUE EGO AGAM POSTHAC
TEMPUS IN OMNE NIHIL.
Anonymous, 1893

Don't mourn for me now, don't
mourn for me ever,
For I'm going to do nothing for
ever and ever!

• 63 •

DIIS IACET HIC FAUSTIS MULIERCULA, CUI SUA VITA
NIL NISI TEMPESTAS UNA FURORQUE FUIT.
HUIC SUPER OSSA LEVIS VESTIGIA PONE, VIATOR,
NE REDEAT FRACTO CLAUSA PROCELLA SOLO.
Translated by Benjamin H. Kennedy, 1850

Here lies, thank Heaven, a woman who
Quarrelled and stormed her whole life through.
Tread gently o'er her mouldering form,
Or else you'll raise another storm.

QUIZ: TEST YOUR LATIN WORDPOWER
——— ANSWERS ———

INFRA DIG
Beneath one's dignity

SIC TRANSIT.
That's how things change.

FLAGRANTE DELICTO
Red-handed

ARIADNE GLADIUM EI DEDIT.
Ariadne gave him a sword.

IN LOCO PARENTIS
In the place of a parent

AB OVO USQUE AD MALA
From beginning to end
(lit. from the egg to the apples)

DE GUSTIBUS NON EST DISPUTANDUM.
There's no accounting for tastes.

NE PLUS ULTRA
Perfection
(lit. nothing past it)

DUM SPIRO, SPERO.
Where there's life, there's hope.
(lit. while I breathe, I hope.)

PER ARDUA AD ASTRA
Through adversity to the stars

NOTA BENE.
Note well.

AUT CAESAR AUT NIL
All or nothing
(lit. Caesar or nothing)

CAVEAT EMPTOR.
Let the buyer beware.

ACKNOWLEDGEMENTS

All translations by Lea Chambers, with the exception of those kindly provided by the following people: Tim Ades, Quintin V.S. Bach, Lynda Goss, Jasper Griffin, David Harvey, W.G. Hoff, Mary Holtby, J.F. Hudson, Matthew Macleod, Mark Mortimer, Jackie Murphy, Keir Page, B.W. Robinson, Margaret Rowley and Alec Taylor.

Extracts on pages 40 and 42 from *Alice in Wonderland* by Lewis Carroll, and *Alicia in Terra Mirabili*, translated from the work of Lewis Carroll by Clive Harcourt Carruthers, are reproduced by kind permission of Macmillan Children's Books, London. With thanks to Mr Graham Carruthers and Miss Janet Carruthers. Latin translation © Clive Harcourt Carruthers 1964.

Extracts on title verso and half title page from *Against Nature* by J.K. Huysmans, translated by Robert Baldick are reproduced by kind permission of Penguin Books, London. Translation © Robert Baldick 1959.

The editors gratefully acknowledge the kind assistance of Dr Jenny March, publicity officer for The Classical Association and editor of *CA News*. We would also like to thank Brian Bishop, Kristina Blagojevitch, Ken Booth, Iain Campbell, Jennifer Capper, Nicola Carr, Stephen Chambers, Mel Menelaou and Tania Shedley.

The editors gratefully acknowledge permission to reproduce illustrations from *Heck's Pictorial Archive of Art and Architecture*, edited by J.G. Heck, published by Dover Publications, Inc. Copyright © Dover Publications, Inc. 1994.

CLASSICAL ASSOCIATIONS

There is a large number of organisations around the world for people interested in the Classics. We have listed just a few key societies, but via these, and the Internet, you can gain access to many more.

AUSTRALIA

The Friends of Antiquity
c/o Dept. of Classics and Ancient
History
Level 7
Michie Building
University of Queensland Q 4072
Telephone: 07 3365 2633
http://www.uq.edu.au/classics/
fantiq2.htm

IRELAND

The Classical Association of Ireland
c/o Professor Andrew Smith
Department of Classics
University College Dublin
Dublin 4
http://www.ucd.ie/~classics/ClassicsIreland.html

SCOTLAND

The Classical Association of Scotland
c/o The Treasurer
Dr Karen Stears
Department of Classics
University of Edinburgh
David Hume Tower
George Square
Edinburgh EH8 9JX
(e-mail) Karen.Stears@ed.ac.uk
http://www.gla.ac.uk/Library/CAS/

ENGLAND

The Classical Association
Dr Jenny March
PO Box 38
Alresford
Hants SO24 0ZQ
Telephone: 01962 773 314
http://www.bigyell.com/ca/

The Society for the Promotion of
Roman Studies (Roman Society)
Secretary, Dr Helen Cockle
c/o The Institute of Classical Studies
Senate House
Malet Street
London WC1E 7HU
Telephone: 0171 862 8727
Fax: 0171 862 8728
(e-mail) romansoc@sas.ac.uk
http://www.sas.ac.uk/icls/roman/

Society for the Promotion of Hellenic
Studies (Hellenic Society)
Secretary, Miss Jane Fisher
c/o The Institute of Classical Studies
Senate House
Malet Street
London WC1E 7HU
Telephone/fax: 0171 862 8730
(e-mail) hellenic@sas.ac.uk
http://www.sas.ac.uk/icls/hellenic/

Friends of Classics
Mrs Jeannie Cohen
Executive Secretary & Treasurer
51 Achilles Road
London NW6 1DZ
Telephone/fax: 0171 431 5088

CANADA

The Classical Association of Canada/
Société canadienne des études classiques
c/o Professor Craig Cooper
Treasurer
Department of Classics
University of Winnipeg
515 Portage Avenue
Winnipeg, Manitoba
Canada R3B 2E9
(e-mail) craig.cooper@uwinnipeg.ca
http://ivory.trentu.ca/www/cl/cac/

USA

The American Classical League
Miami University
Oxford
OH 45056-1694
Telephone: 513 529 7741
Fax: 513 529 7742
(e-mail)
AmericanClassicalLeague@muohio.edu.
http://www.umich.edu/~acleague/

USEFUL SITE ...

For many useful links visit:
The Classical Page at Ad Fontes
Academy

http://patriot.net/~lillard/cp/#links